Corners of the Heart

My Life in Words

Denise D. Rice

Order this book online at www.trafford.com
or email orders@trafford.com

Most Trafford titles are also available at major online book retailers.

Print information available on the last page.

ISBN: 978-1-4907-6564-8 (sc)
ISBN: 978-1-4907-6565-5 (e)

Trafford rev. 10/06/2015

 www.trafford.com

North America & international
toll-free: 1 888 232 4444 (USA & Canada)
fax: 812 355 4082

Contents

Dedication

For Malik, Caleb, Da'Mia, Damarcus,
Devlynn, Lela, Le'Jon, Namon and Willie

A Better Place

(Dedication to Gramps)

Do not cry now that I'm gone,

I'm in a better place, for I am not alone.

I see people I know or once knew,

I am here with my family, it's just a few.

I cherished the days of when I was there,

We'll see each other again so don't be in despair.

I love my family, friends and everyone,

For I'm in a better place I'm not alone.

A Mother

What is a mother that seems to be the question?

She's much like a sister and you have a lot of fun.

She's been there for you through good and bad times,

No one can ever take her place because she's one of a kind.

Everyone has a mother, whom they know they can trust,

I love my mother with all my heart I love her very much.

Whenever you need your mother she's always there,

Those curfews and punishments showed that she cared.

You'll always be my mother no matter what you say,

Forever I will love you each and every day!

A New Love

I found a new love and now I have so much joy,

He's made me see the joys of a team that made of a
girl and a boy.

He listens to me and understands my thoughts,

I smile when I see him because I love the cards he's
bought.

He's one of a kind and different in a way,

He's his own person so what more can I say.

When we go out we have a good time,

He's not only a companion but a good friend of mine.

I often wonder where did he come from, I guess I'll
never know,

I hope he never leaves me and I never let go!

A True Friend

A true friend is there whenever you need them,

They're there for you always as long as don't deceive them.

You've been through good times and both bad times together,

You've told each other secrets to one another.

You knew their ways, you knew their thoughts and you knew what they were going to do,

You knew what they're going to say because they were always true.

When they needed your help you were always there,

If not in person, but in spirit you thought of them in prayer.

So what I'm saying or trying to say,

Sweet wishes and much happiness throughout the day!

African Queen

I am black, sexy, colorful with an excellent stride,

I am an example of that sweetness like hot apple pie.

No one can tell me a thing for I already know enough,

I am not your kid so please don't touch!

I have been beaten, cursed and even accused,

For you cannot take my strength I just plain our refuse.

I am treasured by many and thought of by some,

I see now, what you were jealous of.

I come in different shades, forms and fashion,

Everything I do, I do it with passion.

Now don't get mad at me because I am so truthful,

My attitude, my nature, my skin, now that's beautiful.

I am a mother and a sister, see what I mean,

I'm a dedicated wife and a lover and truly an African
Queen.

Death

Death is a heartache that no doctor can heal,

But loving you as a friend is something no one can steal.

You wasn't that close to me as you were to my
brother,

But I still cared for you, just like I did any other.

But right now I'm still confused trying to find
comforting words to say,

I remember every time I saw your smile it brightened
my day!

As I sit here thinking of you, a tear rolls down my face,

I know that your troubles are at ease, for you're in a
better place.

Another day has come and your memories linger on,

A part of my love went with you, you did not go alone.

Down N' Out

When you're down and out or in dismay,

You know there is a problem, but also a brighter day.

When it looks like things aren't going to make amends,

Just talk to someone call your best friend.

When your job has laid you off and put life on hold,

Don't let them see you down be brave, courageous
and bold.

When you're down and out and feeling sort of blue,

It's nice to know that you have friends that are true.

When your bills are overdue and you don't have the
money,

Even though your behind just be glad you have food in
your tummy.

When you're down and out don't worry your pretty
little mind,

Just thank the man above that you're still alive.

Emotions

When emotions run high you say things you regret,

You told some lies that you won't forget.

You've hurt each other as though it seems,

You've told each other about your dreams.

You've suffered from each other's pain,

Seems like you are taking our love in vain.

We both had ideas in what we wanted to share,

But our emotions got in the way, now you don't care.

It's time to say you're sorry and you always cared,

That feeling of love was always there.

Eternity

I thought I had lost you, but that was only a dream,

For what was weeks it felt like a year as it seems.

When we were apart I went through a living hell,

I knew after I saw you again everything would be well.

I think I know what the word love means,

We go together like two pods and some peas.

As we go on and travel this long journey,

For I'll never hurt you and you'll never hurt me.

So I Love You and you Love me,

And that's the way it will be for all eternity.

Feelings of Anger

I hate I even met you or even saw your face,

Next time I find a man it will be in the right place.

You say things that make me mad and even want to cry,

I look in the mirror and ask myself why?

You've taken me through a lot for reasons I don't know,

My feelings for you have changed my heart maybe so.

The things you do, the things you say, I don't know
  how much more I can take,

I loved you so and you knew, but was your love fake?

Maybe I'll get over you in time I'll see,

For a love that was so strong why did it happen to me?

Feelings

What are feelings I really don't know,

Is it that trust in your friendship while you watch it grow?

What are feelings does it resemble love?

Is it trust, happiness and dependability are all of the
above.

When you're feeling down and sort of blue,

Hope you weren't the type that thought your feelings
wouldn't get you.

Your feelings can express just how you feel,

It's your choice to express them it's you own free will.

So just remember feelings are emotions and don't let
them rise,

For your feelings will be hurtful and you'll say things
just to despise.

Forever My Baby

Forever my baby at least that's what you said last
week,

Till you caught me with my ex and you almost freaked.

It hurt you so bad you didn't know what to do,

When I saw your face all I could say is baby I love you.

You told me that some things was going to change I
took it as a joke,

Then I saw you at the mall with her I nearly choked.

You loved me so much I guess I never really knew,

Now I'm down and out, but yet I still have the blues.

Yes, I wanted to play the field to see just what was out
there,

I know your love for me is shattered it can't be
repaired.

Like the saying goes oh yes there other fish in the sea,

But there will never be another love meant for me.

Forget Him

Forget his smile forget his face,

Forget that warm sweet embrace.

Forget those memories that you once shared,

Forget those feeling that showed you cared.

Forget his ways and that sexy walk,

Forget his presents and that sweet talk.

Forget those places that you use to go,

Forget all of that hearsay, now you know.

Forget those word he use to say,

Forget you ever loved him and went out of your way.

Forget him now because it was never true,

Forget he said those three words I Love You!

God

Goodness and Mercy I pray will follow me.

Obey the commandments and your elderly to.

Don't be disobedient or you will be through.

Help Yourself

Help yourself don't depend on others,

You're always depending on someone else you're just
like your brother.

You're on your own so do the best that you can,

You're your own person even your own man.

Just believe in yourself and you can do anything that
you want,

Always have trust and faith and you'll be successful
just like your Aunt.

There's no such word as the words I can't,

You have a lot on your mind remember love not hate.

Remember that phrase where there's a will there's
a way,

You're on your own so get stronger and live day by day.

I fell In Love With.......

I fell in love with your sweet embrace,

And your beautiful smile and sexy face.

Your sex appeal and the way you talk,

The comfort and ease in your confident walk.

I fell in love with your sweet tenderness,

Your kind heart and soft caress.

And the thought of just seeing you,

Made my heart skip a beat or two.

I fell in love with your spirit and hope,

To lose your love I could not cope.

For not seeing you again, I would be in pain,

My clear sunny days would go from sunshine to rain.

I fell in love with you from the start,

People told me different, I followed my heart.

Look at me, I'm lost without you,

I guess all of the above was just not true!

Jesus

Just believe in him everything will be alright.

Eat and pray every night.

Shout and rejoice if you feel like it.

Use your heart for he will always guide you.

Stay with the Lord and you might like him.

Lies

You tell me lies each and every day,

You tell so many I don't know what to say.

Each lie is different it's never the same,

I never know when it's the truth you think it's a game.

You tell me one thing and you say another,

You say that you care and I ask why bother?

Why can't you tell the truth maybe just once in your life?

Forget the lies and everybody will like you even if they gripe.

Why do you lie no one knows the reason,

You're always lying even through the four seasons.

I can't go on listening to your lies day by day,

Just can't sit around hearing what you have to say.

Life

Life can be cruel in so many ways,

Life can bring happiness so cherish the days.

Life is exciting and can bring new things,

Life is hearing a baby bird sing.

Life isn't easy as though it seems,

Life is full of sunshine and faces with gleam.

Life can be beautiful just wait you'll see,

Life is plain and simple to you and me.

Life isn't always fair you might just get cheated,

Life has its ups and down so don't be greedy.

Loneliness

Why you are alone no one ever knows,

That emptiness in your heart it grows and grows.

To have someone to talk to can make you very glad,

When you're alone and scared you can be oh so sad.

The man you love was caring and true,

But since you stood up as a woman he's turned
   against you.

When you're really alone you have time to think,

You're just like an alcoholic you want a drink.

Nobody ever has to be alone if only they knew,

The man up above will always be there for you!

Love Hurts

Why does love hurt it begins with the heart,

It was love at first sight a new friendship from the start.

You thought you knew him but your thought was wrong,

The love you once shared, now it's gone.

So I ask myself what happened to those lovely endings,

I guess in my heart I was only pretending.

Love can be painful in so many ways,

Someday you'll find the right one so live day by day.

I'm tired of arguing, fighting and such,

All I know is I loved you so much.

Married Woman Blues

I got those blues that people sing about,
The pain and the sorrow and a lot of clot.
Our dating was fun and the marriage was cool,
I'm beginning to feel like a onetime fool.
The married woman blues when I'm with you,
The love is gone and the pain is true.
I prayed to God to send me a man,
And our vows said it all that was the plan.
We don't cuddle, touch, laugh or even play,
I'm losing my love for you each and every day.
The married woman blues when I'm with you,
The love is gone and the pain is true.
The married woman blues when I'm with you
We were like a king and his queen upon the throne,
Now it seems like I'm always alone.
A fairytale romance that's what it was at first,
Now another marriage gone down the tubes what a
    bad, bad curse.
The married woman blues when I'm with you,
The love is gone, and the pain is true,
The married woman blues when I'm with you.

My Best Friend

(Dedicated to Lela Faye)

When I was born, I did not know,

How much your love would grow and grow.

Even though I'm grown and 200 miles away,

You're in my prayers and thoughts every day.

You're my sister, best friend and
mother rolled into one,

I'm grateful for everything that you've said and done!

I didn't want to buy a card because
mine are so much better,

I can add my own feeling and then
you'll burst out in laughter!

You're my mom and my dad for
that I love you very much,

This is a poem dedicated to you with a special touch!

My Dogs and Me

(Dedicated to Spot & Pepe)

My dogs and I were really great friends,

We've been together through thick and thin.

My dogs were friendly and a sight to see,

**When I came home from a long
day they would greet me.**

My dogs and I we grew through the years,

**I remember when they were pups I
use to play with their ears.**

My dogs and I we're like sisters and brothers,

Seeing and playing with one another.

My dogs are in Heaven and has their golden bones,

My house is so quiet for they are not at home!

Peace

Peace is happiness and being cool,

Peace is joyfulness when you're graduating school.

Peace is in the Heavens from up above,

Peace is beautiful when you see a white dove.

Peace is having beauty within in yourself,

Peace is knowing that you have food on your shelf.

Peace is looking at the little birds play,

Peace is going to church and knowing we must pray.

Peace is not just a word that we have to say,

Peace we all need in this world today!

Racism

There is still racism here on this earth today,

There's so much hatred on the other races we all must pray.

What can we do there is no solution,

It's so much prejudice in the world it's just plain pollution.

We all were put on this earth to love one another,

But as it is going now, we're killing each other.

We must face the facts and learn the truth,

Leaving understanding and guidance for our youth.

P.S.

Peace is the answer! We must wake up people!

That Cricket

That cricket chirps all day and night,

It chirps in the morning letting me know all will be alright.

That cricket chirps to find a mate of some kind,

In hopes of not being alone, but having a piece of mind.

That cricket chirps as a form of singing,

It reminds you of a telephone that keeps ringing and ringing.

That noise can be annoying all day long,

It makes you wish that chirper was gone.

How does he do it make such a sound?

While it hops and jumps all over the ground.

A small creature on this earth for us to see,

God put it here for you and me!

The Country -vs- The City

The Country is quiet and you're free as can be,

The City is big with different things to see.

The people are different they grow their own food,

The people in the city eat on the go and sometimes
rude.

You see animals and flowers which are beautiful to
the touch,

A weekend in the city, you will miss it very much.

There's clean and fresh air that you and I can smell,

In the city there's pollution and really loud church bells.

I love the country it's a beautiful place to go,

While staying in the city you can take in a broad way
show.

The Girls

(Dedicated to my God-Daughters)

Denise is sweet and crazy as can be,

Tabatha is sly and smart for both you & me.

Tabatha is provocative and in it for the long haul,

Denise makes you laugh while shopping in a mall.

Denise is calm takes everything at ease,

Tabatha gets what she wants all she says is please.

Tabatha is of age she goes to school every week,

While Denise stays at home with her dimpled cheeks.

Two sweet little girls you'd ever want to see,

With two loving parents their names are Paul and Cathy.

The One You Love

The one you love is right before your eyes,

At night I'm reminded of your laughter and the sound of my cries.

We are apart now and it seems we've went our ways,

I've waited for this moment to see you now it's only a few days.

My feelings for you they haven't changed,

I've been through a lot and that only brought me pain.

I won't hold back my feelings for when I do see you,

Because deep down in my heart they were always true.

We've had some good and bad memories that we have shared,

I ask you do you love me and you say yes I still care.

I've grown up now and now I know,

For if I had you again I'd let my love grow.

There Is Hope

There is hope if you just give it time,

If you just believe everything will be fine.

So don't get down or feeling blue,

Because hope is there it will soon find you.

Don't get discouraged or do things you'll regret,

Because you will find trouble and that's a bet!

If your feelings are down and you're in doubt,

Just raise your head and go about.

Your friends are down and just can't cope,

Tell them there's a better way and just say no.

Things aren't going well and you just don't know,

Just say a little prayer and remember there is hope.

Thinking of You

Just got to thinking of you,

As I often do,

Then started wondering how you've been,

And how things are with you,

So I thought it might be kind of nice,

To send a line you way,

To show I'm thinking of you

And to say "hello" today!

To Be Loved

To be loved is a wonderful feeling,

It's that same type of feeling as if you're in church
singing.

To be loved there are all types of reasons,

That feeling of love changes through months, years
and seasons.

To be loved some people think it's cool,

When that person says I Love You, are you being fooled?

To be loved and to know it you will be very elated,

Those feelings and memories are still there from the
time you dated.

To be loved is a moment that will be treasured for days,

Your memories and feelings will remain always.

To be loved is fun right from the start,

You always prayed you would be together and not apart.

True Love

How do you know when you're really in love,

Is it in your heart or from the man up above?

Love is in your eyes, heart and your soul,

Does the blood in your body turn hot or cold?

When that special person comes around you what do
you do,

Do you stare at him or kiss or say I Love You.

If you are in love you will find out soon,

On the first date you looked at the stars and not the
moon.

You hope it's the person that you've been looking for,

Who can give you love and so much more.

When you think it's love and you get that beat in your
heart,

Ask yourself was it True Love from the very start?

Trust

I trusted you today and I'll trust you tomorrow,

I've put my heart and soul in this relationship so don't
cause me no sorrow.

You want me to trust you, but how can I do that,

When you're not at home, I don't know where you're at!

I love it when we're together and doing things that we
like,

We don't even complain, fuss or fight.

I miss you when you're gone,

I wish that you were home.

You ask me if I'm true, while you are away,

How can I play around I'm at work all day.

Trust is something that you must earn,

I'm in love with you my heart still yearns.

Why

Why do the good people go?

I guess we'll never know.

Why does life deal you a bad hand?

It's just something that we'll never understand!

Why do we have these black & white issues and then
blame it on others?

We should stop killing & fighting and love one another!

Why is there so much hatred & prejudice in the world?

Love every woman, man, boy and girl.

Why is the thought of loneliness such a painful feeling?

Just pray to the Lord and he'll give you your healing.

You Gave Me...

You gave me a new feeling about myself,

You told me I could feel happy and didn't need all that wealth.

You spent time with me and showed that you cared,

Even though you're leaving you told me you'd always be there.

I never believed in true love at first,

Now I know I can't have you that makes things worst.

I have so much fun when I'm with you,

These feelings that I have I know they are true.

You gave me hope in terms of the future,

Because the way I feel now I wouldn't want to lose you.

Jesus

Just believe in him everything will be alright.

Eat and pray every night.

Shout and rejoice if you feel like it.

Use your heart for he will always guide you.

Stay with the Lord and you might like him.

Your Feelings

You're always complaining and saying I don't have this,

But always buying things for yourself like you're rich.

You always have your hands out and want me to give,

Some things are going to change, this mess must end.

You say I talk to you any kind of way,

But if you stop doing certain things I wouldn't have
anything to say.

You want to be the man and play the manly role,

Then pay all of the bills around the house and make
this place a home.

So step up to the plate and be all you can be,

Because those feelings you have mean nothing to me!

Your Thoughts

Your thoughts about me are touching and there's no
doubt,

Sometimes I don't know what your thoughts are about.

Your thoughts are true and very dear to me,

For the love that we share it will always be.

Your thoughts are kind and sweet and such,

That is why I love you so much.

Your thoughts are praised and brings me joy,

My feelings I can't hide they're no decoy.

Your thoughts are truly one of a kind,

For a person like you no one will ever find.

Your Trust

Your trust is gone it's out the door,

I'm beginning not to love you anymore.

I open my heart and show you my love,

You don't return it just because.

You say I'm the only one, but I have my doubts,

When I come home from work you're out and about.

I've seen plenty of movies of how love is suppose to be,

But when you come home to relax it's not with me.

Trust is earned not just something you can buy,

If you give me your heart you'll understand why.

Trust is important in a long-lasting relationship,

But it seems lately all you want to do is trip.

So take heed young man and do all you can,

After all, trust is earned it's in the marriage plan!